Creativity in
the Elementary School

CURRENT PROBLEMS IN EDUCATION

Edited by WILLIAM H. BURTON

IMPROVING READING IN THE JUNIOR HIGH SCHOOL
   By L. Jane Stewart, Frieda H. Heller, and Elsie J. Alberty, *all of Ohio State University.*

HELPING TEACHERS UNDERSTAND PRINCIPALS
   By Wilbur A. Yauch, *Northern Illinois University*

THE USE OF INSTRUCTIONAL MATERIALS
   By Amo de Bernardis, *Portland, Oregon Public Schools* *(in preparation)*

IMPROVING THE ARITHMETIC PROGRAM
   By Leo J. Brueckner, *formerly University of Minnesota*

WORKSHOPS FOR TEACHERS
   By Mary A. O'Rourke, *Massachusetts State Teachers College at Salem,* and William H. Burton, *formerly Harvard University*

GROWING FROM INFANCY TO ADULTHOOD
   By Edward C. Britton and J. Merritt Winans, *both of Sacramento State College*

THE ELEMENTARY SCHOOL CHILD AND HIS POSTURE PATTERNS
   By Evelyn A. Davies, *Indiana University*

UNDERSTANDING MENTALLY RETARDED CHILDREN
   By Harriet E. Blodgett and Grace J. Warfield, *both of The Sheltering Arms, Minneapolis*

CREATIVITY IN THE ELEMENTARY SCHOOL
   By Miriam E. Wilt, *Temple University*

COUNSELING IN THE PHYSICAL EDUCATION PROGRAM
   By Rosalind Cassidy, *University of California, Los Angeles*

ADMINISTRATIVE THEORY
   By Daniel E. Griffiths, *Teachers College, Columbia University*

Creativity in the Elementary School

by

Miriam E. Wilt

TEMPLE UNIVERSITY

NEW  YORK

Appleton-Century-Crofts, Inc.

To the Reader

THE WRITER does not intend this to be a methods book. Its intent is to express a point of view (a philosophy) about creative expression as a basic ingredient of the modern elementary school program. She has attempted to point out the common denominators of all creative endeavor in the elementary age group — i.e., readiness, activities, media, self-evaluation, and adult acceptance.

As the meeting of individual differences, especially for the gifted, becomes increasingly important no possibility in development dares be overlooked. Creative activity can serve the needs of all children from the genius to the slow learner, the emotionally disturbed to the physically handicapped.

It is further felt that although more and more teachers colleges and education departments are concerned about creativity in the various areas — art, literature, music, the dance, etc. — no point of view which is all-inclusive has been considered. Too many teachers are afraid to let children experiment in these areas because they feel uncomfortable about their own lack of knowledge. Since elementary teachers must of necessity be "jacks of all trades" in the curricular areas they develop skill in these fields, and free expression in the arts suffers. Creative expression in the elementary school is another means of communication, not an artist-training course. The importance of stressing creative expression for communication's sake and of guiding those who seem to have talents for real artistry to professional training is stressed throughout the book.

M. E. W.

Contents

1

Getting Off the Ground

Making allowances for human imperfections, I do feel that in America the most valuable thing in life is possible, the development of the individual and his creative powers.

ALBERT EINSTEIN

THIS CHILD of the dancing foot, the nimble mind, the laughing eye, the hungering heart—he *has*, he *is* the creative spirit. Years of disuse of his imaginative faculties dull the growing edges. Memoriter learning, complete domination, unquestioning submission convert the bubbling, effervescent, spontaneous four-year-old into the compliant, conforming, unimaginative ten-year-old. Conformity itself cannot be treated lightly. It is essential in our society much of the time, but as "all work and no play make Jack a dull boy" so all conformity and no free-wheeling thinking make him an uncreative adult.

In the critical mid-twentieth century in which he lives, business, industry, science, the armed services and the arts all cry for the perpetuation of the creative spirit of early childhood. The once-spirited child becomes a bored adult through the suppression and disuse of his own unique mode of investigation, experimentation, and expression. Freedom to do, to think, to discipline and direct himself is essential for the emergence of creative individuals and for the prevention of a waste of human potentialities.

1

REBEL OR SOLID GOLD CITIZEN?

Children have been taught well—to conform. Have they also been given time and encouragement to make choices, to use their imaginations, and to explore their worlds with their senses? This is, of course, not all of the time—this is just some of the time. For there are laws to be learned and obeyed, processes to be learned, other peoples' rights to be respected, group activities to be carried on. But surely there is some time each day or some time each week for furthering Einstein's idea that the individual's creative potential is important.

IDEAS, FROM WHERE?

The "well of the subconscious" is the repository of all the individual's experiences. The experiences flow into this well to be neglected or forgotten or, if encouraged, to be drawn up as the subject matter of his personal expression. Working with words, or colors, or clay, or body movements, or three-dimensional media, or his voice, or musical and percussion instruments, the child arranges his ideas into pattern selected for the expression of his original thought. Is it necessary to point out why this internalization of experience and this expression of ideas are important? Let us look at some of the immediate goals or outcomes for which we can hope if we provide the time and place and emotional environment necessary for creative activities.

IMPERATIVE NOT ONLY FOR SOCIETY BUT FOR SELF-REALIZATION

All human beings have a fundamental need for change, play, recreation, or it may be called just plain fun. If an attempt is to be made to provide the rhythm necessary for healthy minds and healthy bodies, then one must provide time for work and play and rest. And in addition to muscle hunger, is there not a mental hunger that drives one on to think and solve problems?

A second need which (unlike the first) may serve a purpose for only a few is equally important. For the child the telling his own story in his own way may have great therapeutic value. It may be a chimney to carry away the smoke, an escape valve for the pent-up steam. Joys, sorrows, hurts, angers, fears, loves, hates may build up terrific tensions. Let us give these boys and girls a legitimate, a socially acceptable way to reduce the pressure.

Third, through the child's unique expression one may hope to know and understand him better. More important, perhaps, he may gain increased insight into his own behavior. Finally, his peers reveal themselves to him and he reveals himself to them. One cannot express from deep inside without enriching one's understanding of self and others.

A fourth need is that of aesthetic development. To live richly, fully and appreciatively, one must savor life. It must be rolled around on the tongue, mulled over. As the individual touches, tastes, sees, hears, and experiences great art in all fields he develops a respect for the artist. To experiment with all media of creativity strengthens the respect for the hard work of expressing original thought. There has been too much of passive acceptance, too little of active producing. The appreciation of great art develops criteria against which achievements may be measured. A creative person's own efforts are dignified by what he learns from the masters.

A fifth personal need has to do with thinking—with organizing one's experiences into an orderly sequence saying the thing as only the creator can say it. At individuals struggle to communicate, they are calling into play creative. critical, disciplined thinking that follows the scientific problem-solving sequence. To memorize is temporal; to internalize is lasting.

Cognate with this need to create is the need for the individual to live well with himself. Mauree Applegate suggests that every human being needs a white space in his day—a margin around the multiplicity of activities with which his waking hours are taken up. Thus, it may be the farmer sitting alone under his oak tree, gazing across his acres; the housewife seeking solitude, perhaps where A. A. Milne suggests in his "Halfway Down":[1]

[1] From the book *When We Were Very Young* by A. A. Milne. Copyright, 1924, by E. P. Dutton & Co., Inc. Renewal, 1952, by A. A. Milne. Reprinted by permission of the publishers.

Halfway down the stairs
Is a stair
Where I sit.
There isn't any
Other stair
Quite like
It.
I'm not at the bottom,
I'm not at the top;
So this is the stair
Where
I always
Stop.

or as Beatrice Schenk de Regniers suggests in a small book called *A Little House of Your Own*. In this book the child is introduced to the concept that everybody needs a place where he can get away by himself, away from everybody and everything; and "if *you* should be walking near somebody's little house remember to be very polite—walk softly—speak gently"[2] so as not to disturb whoever is there.

And again, Anne Morrow Lindbergh in *Gift from the Sea*:

Perhaps we never appreciate the here and now until it is challenged, as it is beginning to be today even in America. And have we not also been awakened to a new sense of the dignity of the individual because of the threats and temptations to him, in our time, to surrender his individuality to the mass—whether it be industry or war or standardization of thought and action? We are now ready for a true appreciation of the value of the here and the now and the individual.[3]

To each his own island. It is these frames or white spaces that provide the time to organize experiences for expression; or again, in the words of Miss Applegate: "Periods of peace are necessary for the creation of stable lives and for the growth of

[2] Beatrice Schenk de Regniers and Irene Haas, *A Little House of Your Own* (New York: Harcourt, Brace and Company, 1954), (pages unnumbered).

[3] Anne Morrow Lindbergh, *Gift from the Sea* (New York: Pantheon Books, Inc., 1955), p. 127.

talents."[4] Perhaps if we teach children "to seek a quiet time alone each day . . . they will not become adults who have a horror of being alone with themselves."[5]

Let us take another—a longer—look at these potential creative faculties in a child:

His Dancing Feet

Running, jumping, skipping, balancing, swaying, dancing, and swinging. He chooses his movements as the artist chooses his colors. He combines them into his own patterns and they are his. Sometimes he creates in response to external rhythms; sometimes his internal timing controls his movements, and others pick up the beat with strings or drums or bugles. Gloriously free, he dances until he drops from sheer exhaustion. He is telling a story with his body. His body is singing a lovely song. From mining coal to picking cotton, his lively nimble foot is telling you his story.

His Probing Hand

Life is "stuff"—his hand must knead it and shake it, poke it and punch it, smooth it and fondle it. He must tuck it away in his pocket, that scrap of crimson satin or emerald velvet, to hold against a lonely moment. He must smooth his puppy's coat and lightly touch the rose petal. He must explore the texture of driftwood and of rough oak bark. He must hold the snowflake in his hand and crush the paper. But his hand does more—it holds the pencil or brush or clay that tells his story. The hand records the joy, the sorrow, the beauty, the pathos aroused by his senses.

His Questing Mind

The everlasting "whys" of childhood. He finds answers to his questions by looking, listening, reading, and experimenting. His mind is so full of "wanting to know" that it scarcely seems that one small cranium could hold so much. It's a creative

4 Mauree Applegate, *Everybody's Business—Our Children* (Evanston, Illinois: Row Peterson and Co., 1952), pp. 220, 221.
5 *Ibid.*, p. 220.

experience when he watches the water turn to steam and the steam to water. It's creative when he rigs the wheel that turns the belt that makes the paddle go. And it's creative when he goes to a book to find answers to his questions. The whole wide world is there to be explored, manipulated, prodded, made to give back its secrets. Can one set these children free to discover the things they need to know? Can teachers help them acquire the skills that make it possible for them to learn? The Einsteins and Salks and Tennessee Williamses are there in your classrooms, often begging to be set free.

His Hungering Soul

He fears awesomely, hates lustily, loves explosively, supports courageously, defends loyally. His volatile emotions rise and swell and fall as the tides of the ocean. There is no sign of lethargy in his feelings toward people and experiences. He grieves and hopes and despairs. Joy pervades his every motion and word, as does sorrow. As transient as April showers, as necessary as summer rain, his moods color his days and hours. The creative individual feels deeply. His most effective creative endeavors are emotionally spark-plugged. Intense emotions parade across his life as pictures on a screen.

His Mercurial Voice

Sometimes strident; often loud, laughing, sighing; sometimes crying. It shrieks with joy and screams with pain; and throughout childhood, from dramatic play to sociodrama, he plays upon his voice as the musician plays upon his instrument. "I am Father Bear and I am Baby Bear." Through poetry reading, story telling, creative dramatics he plays out his role as a giant, a wicked step-mother, or a lovely Cinderella. He hums before he can talk, he laughs, he sings, he shouts, he whistles, and with each activity he releases some of his pent-up energy and often his feelings.

His Spirit

Each of us must be his best self, not all of the time but some of the time. Lest we lose ourselves in mediocrity we must find ourselves. What does conformity mean? Is there no place in our society for the individual? It's a delicate balance that must be achieved. To be one's own unique self and yet to be an acceptable group member, to be strong but flexible, to be sensitive to others. To know when conformity protects and when uniqueness pays is a worthy goal. And the end-product is self-discipline, self-direction, and order.

WHAT ARE THE MEDIA OF CREATIVITY?

We create with words—fragments of sentences, poems, stories, essays; in dramatic play, creative dramatics, choral speaking; in songs, operas, operettas, and ballads.

We create with our bodies—in dance, rhythm, games, sports, and calisthenics.

And we create with our hands—with pencils, crayons, paints, cut paper; with wire, tin foil, and solder; with cloth and wood and food. We sew, we dance, we saw, we hammer, we cook. There is no material that cannot be used creatively, have we only the eye to see and the mind to weave a magic spell.

BEGINNING, WHERE?

But where to begin? How shall we start to use what we know? *You can't and should not try to teach creative expression.* What then, you ask, is your role? What use is a teacher who does not teach? You are the catalyzer, the element that makes self-expression possible. If you can free children to dig deep in the well of their subconscious, to bring to the surface those ideas, thoughts, dreams, pictures, tunes—you will be giving these children a priceless heritage. And in addition to not selling children short, you will be serving yourself well. You will earn a dividend—a bonus, if you like—a tangential value that is sought by all teachers. As children find their safety valves—as self-control, self-discipline, self-direction increase through creative activities—the need for extrinsic disciplinary measures tends to decrease and often to disappear.

GETTING OFF THE GROUND

First, you must believe that if a child is really to create something it must grow out of frequent opportunities to experiment and grope for his own best way to express his idea. Permitting him to grope is the one best way to gain self-knowledge. In groping toward an end-result that satisfies him, about which he can say "It is mine. It is good. I like it." he finds self-realization. Working in his own way, following his own desires, fumbling as he goes, he must approve of his own work.

The role of the teacher in the area of creative activities is quite different from that of curricular guidance. Here there is no right or wrong, no good or bad as such. Here the teacher must be willing neither to teach nor to judge. The creator gropes for his own way to do and makes his own judgment of the quality of his product. In deep humility the teacher must accept the realization that this is a "hands-off" business, that other than the verbal help of asking questions that encourage the child along the lines of his own thinking, any help is nebulous. An emotionally healthy climate, a rich environment, and verbal support are all that should be supplied.

The teacher should accept enthusiastically and generously whatever personal expression the child dreams up. Regardless of the creative result, he must always realize that the process is of far more consequence than the product.

Finally, the teacher should be insightful enough to keep alive the child's ideas and not tamper with an individual's personal expression. He must value above all the original idea, the unique invention, the vigorous lucid individual effort. The expression of ideas must always take precedence over correct form. The teacher must be honest and have enough integrity never, never to betray or violate a confidence.

Into the well of the subconscious, we have said, flow all of the experiences and it is from this well that the creator draws up his ideas. Thus the richer the living, the more the individual will have to draw from. The first step then is a rich experiential background.

A by-product of this experiencing should be rich sensory

activities. Children often must learn that having strong feelings and expressing them is acceptable—senses are alerted through tasting, smelling, touching, seeing, hearing. Life must be savored in all of its beauty, its starkness, its sorrow, pain and grief, its joy and courage. Children must be shown that their reactions to the sensory world are worthwhile. There's more in Jimmy's "Them clouds look like fluffy pink kittens" than a usage error. There's something of value in "How do you feel when you're happy?" . . . "I feel like my mouth is jokey and wants to laugh." or "You look like a tall glass of cool cocoa."

The picturesque language of young children is often so musical and rhythmic that it might well be called poetry. Life is so enchanting and new and exciting that they reach out to enfold each experience with all of their sensory equipment. In verbalizing these experiences their language is unique and ingenious.

By the same token their bodies respond with the same delightful uniqueness in the dance, and their modeling and painting reveal nothing of the stereotyped expression of later childhood. They commence as free spirits; which path they follow will to a great extent be determined by the teachers they meet.

Concurrent with and prior to actual creative activities there should be exposure to great art in all of its forms. There is no room for the shoddy, the trite, the cheap. Give them a generous dosage of fine literature—poetry, fiction and other prose; of well-chosen masterpieces in painting, sculpture, ballet, symphonic and operatic music. This is not creative expression—this is their cultural heritage, their birthright, and it belongs in their daily programs. Out of these rich aesthetic experiences standards for their own products are developed. Respect for the original ideas of the creators, respect for the discipline necessary for telling one's own story, will be valuable adjuncts to the values inherent in appreciation of both the visual and "listened-to" variety.

Stories, poems, paintings, movies or still pictures, clay figures, or any record of the efforts of children of comparable age shared with youngsters may serve several purposes. First, it gives them an opportunity to evaluate the work of children like themselves in a positive constructive way. It is often a critical point because an attitude of positive acceptance develops with the emphasis on what they *like* about what they see or hear rather than on what is *wrong*. It can establish appreciative acceptance of all creative efforts.

As children experience both in real life and through the arts, they should constantly be talking about what they are seeing and doing. As they grope for words to say it (or in the words of a child, "I have to talk so I know what I think") they are experimenting with symbols and constantly evaluating. This cementing of experience into language symbols helps in the process of enriching and maintaining the experience. This is perhaps what the child meant when he said, "I draw a think and put a line around it." It becomes more truly his as he finds a way to record it.

Looking, touching, tasting, smelling, hearing, doing. Discussing—and suddenly you have arrived. Children either express a wish to try—a story, a poem, a dance—or else they simply start. Carried on by the momentum of their own enthusiasms they "scribble" with any medium that comes to mind or hand. Taking the time to set the stage through rich creative readiness activities should now begin to pay off in children's having something to say, wanting to say it, and knowing that whatever it is it will be graciously and generously accepted both by the teacher and the peer group. In this chrysaline stage the effect of negative criticism may be absolutely devastating. Nothing can so quickly shatter or shut off further efforts as can unenthusiastic comments or ridicule.

Maybe only a half dozen or even less will start, but creativity is as infectious as a cold and will probably grow to epidemic proportions before too long. In the meantime, those not participating will go about their business—the business of being children. They will go about it quietly, because as one child said, "You'll have to keep very quiet inside so that you won't scare away your thoughts."

In this unhurried quiet time of the day children are often filled with wonder and enchantment. As they ponder and muse over the hint of an idea they must have plenty of time to let it simmer. Creation is a slow business, but of one thing you can be certain: the *right* words, forms, shapes, steps, or whatever they seek will come to the surface when they need them.

It is likely that you will introduce creative activities in your classes one at a time. Later as children become proficient with various media many different activities will be going on, but at first—especially if these are new activities for you—they should be introduced gradually. At the end of the time each child's efforts will be shared—will be shared if the child so desires. Sometimes children who have written or painted or even danced in response to deep emotional stimuli are reluctant to have others participate in their experiences. This reluctance should be respected until the child willingly shares. He may wish to confide only in you, and this, too, should be respected.

You and the children should be emotionally prepared to find just the right thing to say to bring to each child the recognition he desires. This is a critical time when overpraise or underpraise may wreck all that has gone before. Comments must be honest, must be sincere. Sometimes it is difficult to reconcile honesty and need, but as your insight increases so will your skill—and if you look hard enough the uniqueness is almost always there.

Children are so eager to please that one of the more difficult aspects of encouragement will be getting them to express themselves in their own way. Children who write or dance or paint in a highly individual manner, who know that what they do doesn't always please everyone, but that you—the teacher—are in there rooting for them, will trust you. If they have confidence in you they don't offer you triteness because they want to please. They know that honesty and sincerity of purpose are what you value and prize. Doing what we like and liking what we do becomes the byword.

Without formal teaching they will begin to sense the psychological value of a good beginning, the rounding out of an idea to a good conclusion, the use of the just right word or color or twist of the wire or movement of the body. Spelling and punctuation will often improve. You will show your joy in their uniqueness, you will ignore their clichés. Our judgment or appraisal as adults is often faulty, often based on too little knowledge, often biased and prejudiced by our own experiences and emotions. It is dangerous to make a judgment which, positive or negative, may like the ripple in the river go on and on. Few of us are art critics or literary geniuses, nor are many of us musically talented. In our humility we admit that we often don't know but we like it because "you know, no one but Johnny could have said it that way." Children will trust you with their most haunting dreads, fears, and horrors when they know that you are on their side.

To the critics of permissiveness you can show independent able people who are self-directing, self-disciplined and self-controlled; you can show them boys and girls willing and able to conform most of the time because they know how to think, how to size up a problem and arrive at a solution—boys and girls willing to conform when it is for their and society's best interest, because they know that there will always be "tomorning," that lovely time when the chains are off. That time when torrents of ideas will surge up from the well deep inside and find their expression in some form of communication, be it music, dance, language, clay or paint.

2

Words Are the Colors on My Palette

For who has sight so keen and strong
That it can follow the flight of song?[1]

How CAN WE catch that ephemeral thought, idea, sentence,
poem, story, or drama? Shall we try—and if so, why? How can
we recognize the unique, the original, the soul-satisfying product? How can we help the child move from where he is to
where he wants to go in his creative-language expression?

The bubbling four-year-old talks and talks and talks. He
dramatizes his environment and human contacts, he reacts to
natural phenomena, he asks a multitude of questions, he tries
out words on his tongue and his ear. He sums up a sensory
snow experience with "powder puffs are on the rose of Sharon
bush" without self-consciousness or fear of rebuff. Surely and
inexorably he moves through the elementary school and just as
surely, in many instances, his wonderful language facility—
rather than continuing to grow in creative ways of expression—
deteriorates into, "The title of my book is Blah-blah. The author
is Blah-blah. The main characters are . . . " and so on ad infinitum. So we ask ourselves: How can we teach conventions to this
bundle of atoms without completely destroying his uniqueness,
his ingenuity, his charming use of language? Thoughtful teachers for many years have tried to solve this riddle, and out of
years of trying have come the generalizations that follow.

[1] Henry Wadsworth Longfellow, "The Arrow and the Song."

IT'S YOU WHO COUNT

Yes, you are his teacher when he is in school. You are responsible for the mastery of skills, for developing attitudes, for expanding understandings, for deepening insights, for increasing factual knowledge. Yes, you are his "drillmaster," but if you do not go beyond that you will miss much of the thrill of teaching. Furthermore, knowledge, attitudes, and skills are best achieved in an atmosphere of mutual respect and understanding —often a natural outcome of creative activities. An emotional climate where unique human beings are valued is one in which there is time and encouragement for Johnny to tell his own story, choosing his own words and arranging them in a sequence that is satisfying to him, often revealing and so many times healing. Yes, it is you who count.

YOU CREATE AN ENVIRONMENT IN WHICH UNIQUENESS IS PRIZED

"You look like a tall glass of cool cocoa" says the six-year-old as she looks lovingly at her tall willowy auburn-haired teacher in her chocolate-brown dress.

To keep this alive, literature is shared, for sooner or later everyone seems to fall into the clichés of "roses are red" unless some understanding adult shares beautiful language with children, from Shakespeare to Hilda Conkling. Prizing, valuing as we go, we constantly bombard these young ears with such a wide variety of interesting language in prose, drama and, poetry that the young dreamer is constantly searching for a way to make his meanings more and more fluent and expressive. Perhaps long before he offers a phrase or a sentence, or perhaps concurrent with expression, he will be savoring and rolling around on his tongue those apt phrases that strike his fancy, tickle his funny bone, or respond with quiet beauty. When he desperately digs deep into his subconscious searching for the right words, he will find them there within himself.

This environment of faith, beauty, and quiet is an intangible —hard to describe, but an essential ingredient of a program that balances necessary conformity with an opportunity to be one-self. This fine balance is achieved only when you create an environment in which each and every individual knows that uniqueness is prized.

CATCH A FALLING STAR

We wish to capture these expressions, not so much to have a record of them, but rather because we want each child to feel the importance of his experiences and his success in the search for words to share these experiences. A child chews on gritty fog, holds a snowflake for a moment, bites into a hard juicy apple, hears the crackle of the snow on a frosty morning, sees a startled doe—and somehow, somehow he must share this wonderful sensory experience. This is the "stuff" of which poetry is made.

Such language pictures as these may evolve:

In the autumn the trees put on their stockings and the colors look like the pile of socks at the store. (*7 years*)

I love Christmas because the good things in people shine through their eyes and smiles. (*7 years*)

Soaked lima beans look old like grandmums and grandpops. (*6 years*)

The rain on the window looks like lots of silver ants. (*5 years*)

I am necklacing the beads. (*4 years*)

These milkweed pods locked their shells tight like pirates guarding chests of silk and gold. (*9 years*)

Icicles are glass needles. (*6 years*)

I was so tired that my shoes were walking on tip-toe. (*5 years*)

When I'm happy, my mouth feels joky and wants to laugh. (*6 years*)

I saw the sun surrounded by fog.
A flock of birds flew past the sun.
Then the flap of wings died away. (*11 years*)

Whenever I think of the ocean I have a strange feeling of standing on a rock near the ocean. It seems I'm the Queen of the Sea
and yet all I can see is me. I seem to be able to feel the ocean
air and hear the waves. When I think of the ocean, everything
seems sad, but very beautiful. Then in an instant the feeling and
picture vanish and I'm left wondering what happened. (*11 years*)

A treasure chest is locked within a crew-cut or pigtailed
cranium, or heart or soul. As fragile as the wings of the
new-born moth, expressions may emerge and live, or shrivel and
die. Perhaps they may never see the light of day or have a
chance to crystallize in the air. You say:

I am only one, and there are so many children. Ah, yes. A
practical problem this. One pair of ears to listen, one pair of
hands to record—and thirty mouths to voice these ephemeral
ideas. It isn't always easy, but all thirty children will never be
dictating at any one time and the creative impulse soon is
conducive to independence. In the meantime, until your charges
can write them themselves, use a tape recorder for some of
their expressions, take down as many as you can—carry a pad
and jot them down as you go. As important as spelling, hand-
writing, and punctuation are in expressing ideas, your concern
here is not with mechanics but with the idea itself. Get it on
paper as best you can, and later see that it is put into acceptable form.

In this phase of creative activity, as in every other, seldom do
all children create at the same time. As a matter of fact, creative
writing is really only for some of the children some of the time.
You and I do not write or paint or weave by the clock. By the
same token in our work with children we can't turn a faucet and
expect to fill a cup. Quiet reflection, appreciative listening may
unleash a flood for a few of the children, but most will wander
into other areas for quiet activities, and the writers will write,
asking only for quietness so that their thoughts will not be
frightened away.

Raindrops fall,
Clouds bump together,
When we have rainy weather.

Children play in puddles
And splash all around
When we have rainy weather. (*6 years*)

The whole country is clammy and cold.
The cold bites through you.
All is very quiet
Except for the chirping of birds
And the occasional caw of a crow. (*11 years*)

When I see a star
I wonder how big it is.
I wonder if a plane can reach it and
If it really is
Bigger than me. (*8 years*)

There is a place in summer time
Where boys like to go.
It may be to the river
To some secret place they know. (*10 years*)

The snow makes me think of popcorn
And cotton coming down—
Spacemen and firemen coming down
Their pole—
White lights, bubbles, marshmallows,
Paper, flying saucers, soap flakes
And periods—
Thousands of little men, parachutes,
The north wind, white mice, birds and stars—
It looks like Indians dancing out of the
Sky and soap bubbles coming down.
The trees have a white coat on.
White fairies, ice cream for you and me,
Flying birds——
It makes me shiver!
I keep thinking the angels are having a
Pillow fight.
It is a dream come true. (*3rd grade*)

THIS COULD HAVE HAPPENED

Writing stories is contagious. Let just one child bring a story and often an epidemic results. They may cast themselves, their friends, their parents, their teachers in animal roles or as inanimate objects. Sometimes they simply use fictitious names. In this kind of anonymity they often get back at authority figures or get the best of bullies. The timid become brave souls. The physically weak are strong.

In their stories they describe life as they see it. The behavior of adults often seems unjust to them, and in story writing they are free to picture justice as they see it. Punishment swiftly follows naughtiness, but the right person gets punished. Fooling nobody—not even themselves—they set the stage so that sanctimonious adults are discomfited. They chuckle with their listeners at the ridiculous spots in which they put adults.

Impudence and impertinence do not always seem like cardinal sins to these neophyte novelists. They often do not even recognize them as socially unacceptable behavior. The shrug of shoulder or tone of voice that drives the adult to a frenzy is often followed by an injured "What did *I* do?" In story writing the child has an opportunity to talk back, to be as tiresome as he pleases, to blow off steam, to let loose his bitterness—because it's not for real . . . he's not really doing the talking . . . it's somebody else saying what he'd like to say, doing what he'd like to do. Into the mouths of his characters he puts the words he dares not utter. He knows the mores, he accepts the code, but unless he uses some sort of escape valve—such as story writing—he may explode where it is important *not* to explode. Many children have these feelings. Story writing may give them a legitimate outlet so that conformity to adult dictates is easier to bear. Often it isn't that they don't know better, but that they are seeking relief from tension—a clearing of the air.

A teacher's insight, too, is deepened as children reveal their real or imaginary grievances, their misunderstanding of certain rules, their likes and dislikes. Adults frequently don't realize how ridiculous they look to children, how unfair their standards seem, how unrealistic their demands appear. Let children hold a mirror up to you and see what is reflected there. You may be right, they may be wrong—but at least you'll both know what the other thinks, and mutual respect may result.

The Baby Who Tried to Work the Telephone

Once upon a time there was a lady and her name was Mrs. Green. One day Mrs. Green had a baby. When the baby was a year old he began to get into trouble.

One day the baby pulled all the labels off the cans. And another day he spilled a bowl of soup. Then one day he saw the telephone. First he thought it was any old toy. He did not like toys. He liked interesting things. Then he saw all the wires and things. He started to mess around with it.

First he lifted the receiver and the operator said, "Number please." The baby was so surprised he threw a glass of water right in the telephone. Then he lifted the receiver again and water squirted in his face.

After that he was never curious again. And as for the telephone, he never bothered that again.

And so they lived happily ever after.   (7 years)

Twelve Tomorrow

Twenty-four hours to go, twenty-four hours to go, one more day to go and I'll be twelve years old. I don't want to get out of bed now; I want to dream, dream, dream about tomorrow. I wonder how it's going to feel to be twelve. Will I be sophisticated, pert, snobbish, cute or just plain me?

"Patsy, Patsy, time to get up!" called Mrs. Bradley above the noise of the radio and the roar of Patsy's father's car as he left for work.

"I'm coming. Don't rush me," laughed Patsy.

Patsy continued to daydream as she got dressed for school. It was May twenty-ninth and tomorrow was a holiday as well as her birthday! It's nice to be famous, to have your birthday acclaimed as a national holiday all over the United States.

She was all dressed now and would have to get washed. She turned on the faucet and listened to the gurgling of the water. She put her hands in the water and felt the good feel of fresh water rolling down her face.

She gathered her school books on the way downstairs and pertly said to her dog, Wamper, "Hello, my darling." She had decided to act sophisticated. Her mother came over to her and asked if she had washed. "You don't look washed to me young lady. Now you march right upstairs and wash your face and teeth and don't you dare forget to make a straight part."

"I am clean, mother."

"No you're not. Now do as I say."

"Well, tomorrow's my birthday."

"Tomorrow you can get away with murder but not today!"

Her mother's speech was interrupted by her older sister's phonograph record, "All I Have to Do is Dream, Dream, Dream."

"Shut that thing off, Madeline Bradley," screamed her mother.

Patsy gulped down some juice and started walking to school. She was in a half-daze as she walked. In a couple of more weeks I'll be in Junior High, she thought, I'll go on dates, go to canteen, and I'll be one of the crowd.

"Hey, Queenie!" shouted Bill. Bill always called her that because she was going to be a burlesque queen. "There's Sarah Heartburn up at the corner," he continued. Amy was Sarah's real name. She was going to be an actress.

"Oh, shut up, Midgie," Patsy replied. Bill was very short and the nickname hurt. They walked to school very slowly. Bill usually walked to school with Amy. Patsy was happy and surprised that Bill was walking with her. She thought she must be more sophisticated already even though her birthday wasn't until tomorrow.

"Queenie, how about going to the movies with me tomorrow?" Bill said. Patsy's heart started pounding. She was all choked up. She managed to squeeze out, "Oh, I'd love to."

They met Amy a block further along and she said to Bill, "Billy, I'm invited to Margie Bell's girl-invite-boy party. Will you go as my escort?"

Bill looked at Patsy. Patsy crossed her fingers as a hint. "Patsy has already invited me," he replied.

"Oh, you're mean, mean, mean," cried Amy and she ran away.

"Oh, we acted awfully mean," said Patsy.

"Hey, you better hurry; there's the first bell," replied Bill.

All day at school nothing eventful happened. The day seemed twice as long as usual. When Patsy got home, she did her homework and read a "Nancy Drew" book. At dinner she didn't eat very much, and she went to bed at seven. She replied to her mother's questioning voice, "If I go to bed early, tomorrow will come quicker, goodnight."   (*11 years*)

FOR SHE NEVER SAW A FAIRY
AT ALL, AT ALL, AT ALL

In and out of the world of fantasy flit these imaginary creatures. "This is a make-believe story," says Polly Pigtails. "Once upon a time . . . " and she is off, spinning a tale that holds her small audience enchanted while marvelous feats of courage are performed, sumptuous feasts are served, ugly ducklings become beautiful princesses, cruel elder sisters or brothers are punished, or wishful dreams are fulfilled. Talking the story or writing the story, the young author paints a rich canvas, often revealing his innermost dreams, fears, or wishes.

Often the story is only told, and is not recorded in writing. But verbal rehearsal gives the young child faith in himself, faith in his ability to use words to make a picture. Hearing themselves tell their own stories often has most rewarding results for children as they clarify their ideas and organize them into a logical sequence.

Little Fleecy

Once there lived in a little village a family of winds. There were seven of them. There was Mama and Papa, Grandma and Grandpa, Aunt and Uncle and Little Fleecy. One morning when Fleecy blew downstairs to breakfast, Mama was talking to the bigger winds.

Mama said, "I think it's time for Fleecy to take blowing lessons. What do you think?"

"I agree," said Fleecy.

"Why Fleecy you were ease-dropping."

"Oh well, it was about me anyway," said Fleecy.

"Fleecy, do you really want to take blowing lessons?"

"Oh yes," replied Fleecy.

"Alright," said Mama, "I'll call up Blowers Blowing School right after breakfast."

Fleecy was excited so he ate only two bowls of Blowy Krispies. After breakfast Mama called, and signed up for Fleecy.

Mr. Blower said, "Send him down right now and I'll give him his first lesson." Mama hung up and got Fleecy ready to go.

Fleecy blew down the street in a hurry. When he got there

Mr. Blower gave him instructions to get in line with the other blowers.

Mr. Blower told him to do what he did. Blowing was pretty hard, at first. Pretty soon School was over.

Mr. Blower told Fleecy, "You know you're the first little wind I had that learned how to blow on his very first lesson." Fleecy was proud of himself.

When he got home he told his mother he never had to go again. And he never did.

And some day when your hat blows off and rolls away remember Little Fleecy.   (*7 years*)

You give children a belief in your integrity if you accept their own impressions. They begin to trust you, and this is the foundation upon which true creative expression is built. Soon, if they know that you will not violate their confidences, they will reveal—in autobiographies—their innermost feelings, wonderings, reactions, and dreams.

A Moment I Would Like to Remember

One moment I'll always remember is the time when three new things entered my life. One was a begonia, one a stuffed elephant, and last but not least a baby sister. This is how it went. One Wednesday morning my father went to the hospital to get my mother while my Nana stayed home with me. At noon the doorbell rang. I ran to open it, a strange sight greeted my eyes. There was my father holding a pink plant with a long name and next to him was my mother holding something pink and red and "cuddly" and in her other arm was a gray ball of fur. My father put down the pot of flowers and then he introduced us to each other. The cuddly thing was my baby sister, who to me looked more like a stuffed doll that was alive. The gray ball of fur was a stuffed animal elephant and the plant looked very pretty to me. This is one of my oldest memories and I will cherish it forever.

❖   ❖   ❖   ❖

I live in a house on Catherine Street. We have two rooms and a bath. There are seven other children in the family besides me. I like to take care of my younger brother and sister. When my mother goes out, she lets me look after them. Sometimes I have to miss school on account of it. I don't like to miss school but then it wouldn't be right to leave two little kids alone. They might get in trouble.

My father doesn't live with us. We don't know where he is. My mother says he walked out one day and never came back. She said he didn't want to be bothered with us. I don't know why he'd do a thing like that.

I love my mother. She works awful hard. I had to stay home with the kids today 'cause she had to go out to find out about some job. She got sick when she had the other one. She had to stay home for awhile until she got better. I hope she'll be alright when she gets a new job. She says she better 'cause we need the money.

It'll be a little better when my sister can get a job. I don't know about her though. The other night she went to a dance and the cops brung her home. It's not good when the cops have to bring you home.

I like to come to school. You can do some good things here . . . like paint. I like it too 'cause sometimes when kids are absent you get an extra bottle of milk. I really love milk . . . it tastes good. We don't have it at home. It costs too much money.

My older brother isn't too good either. He doesn't help my mother like he should.

I worry about my school work. Some of the other kids are brighter than me. I am behind in my work. Maybe when I get up to the fourth grade I'll be able to catch up. I hope I don't have to go to O.B. like my brother Ronald. He says the kids there are silly and mean. They fight a lot. I don't like to fight.

The kids here in school are alright. They fight too much though. They ought to try and get along better. I like to play with them sometimes, not all the times though. They run too much and I get tired trying to keep up.

I like to read and paint. I like to water the flowers too. They'll die if they aren't watered.

ALL THE WORLD'S A STAGE

Before these neophytes can talk they are playing out life. Susan serves us tea from her toy tea set, gravely passes cream and sugar, after which she pretends to wash and dry her dishes. She wraps and unwraps her doll in a handkerchief, cuddles it in

Strings and things — runes and tunes

her arms, gently sways back and forth. She has no need of words, yet! Later, as vocabulary grows, she combines language with action. Mothers, fathers, teachers, see themselves imitated in play before their startled eyes. Tone of voice, personal habits and characteristic expressions are mimicked before them.

Long before many children are comfortable with their own language patterns they are asked to learn lines that someone else has written. Before they reach first grade they are sometimes asked to memorize poems for "saying pieces" or repeat verbatim lines of a play. This is not creative dramatics. This is not what we are talking about. Creative dramatics spring from the inside into body movements and language. Empathy is so strong in true creative dramatics that the actor becomes the character he impersonates. Years later, when this young man is an expert in his own use of language, this empathizing will help him take the words of Shakespeare or Christopher Fry and make them his own.

The child tries on life in his dramatic play. He plays father, mother, doctor, grocer, policeman. He creates his dialogue as he goes. Later he begins playing stories he hears, stories he knows—folk and fairy tales, here-and-now stories, legends, fables and parables. He learns no lines—he makes them, he lives them. Because he uses his own language patterns he knows and understands what he says. Expression is no problem when a child is articulate. As he moves into the middle grades he goes farther afield—he plays long-ago and far-away people. His desire to really be the person he portrays leads him on a treasure hunt for information about the character. He learns how the person lived, what he wore, what he ate, what he did, where he traveled. Out of this information the actor fashions a person, a personality. He experiments with language until it satisfies him and the others involved in the action.

The child's heritage is a rich source of dramatic activities. In history, literature, science, and current affairs he will find his themes, plots or threads. As he emerges from dramatic experiences, you—his teacher—will be gratified to find how much he has gained in vocabulary, factual knowledge, organization of thinking, social skill, insight, and many other intangibles.

A group of children, a wisp of chiffon, a broomstick, a paper hat, a little elbow room, an appreciative enthusiastic teacher— these are the ingredients of elementary school dramatics. Shall we write it down? What does it matter? They are living it. At best the writing of it should serve only as a record of what they have lived.

To Tell Our Story We Chant Together

1.

Girl Solo: What is steel? What is steel- What is steel?

Low: It is the history and development . . .

Middle: The past . . .

High: The present . . .

All: And the future of America!

Low: It is science!

Middle: It is history!

High: It is geography!

All: It is yesterday, today and tomorrow,

It is men and women,

The tools you use, the desk, the chair,

Your school, your home, your community!

Boy Solo: It's the tacks in the heel of your shoe.

Girl Solo: And the clasp on a barrette.

2.

All: It is limestone, iron ore and bituminous coal!

Low: Not the shiny stainless steel?

All: It is work, with hands and tools!

In the mines, a thousand feet down.

Anywhere they strike a vein of coal

Man must *first!* shoulder the load!

He must labor in the foundry, he must withstand the heat of the steel. He must worry, tired and dirty, for fear he can't pay his bills!

Girl Solo: So to make his burden lighter he sings,

He sings! He sings! He sings!

All: And what does he sing?

Girl Solo: He sings about his work, his problems,

his joys and sorrows,

And this my friends . . .

Has given us many legends. Our heritage.

Boy Solo: I am John Henry!

All: What! John Henry, the steel driving man?

3.

All: Sing John Henry (*as he swings heavy mallet*)

All: Problems! Problems! Problems!

Bible Quotation: "Yet man was born to troubles
          as the sparks fly upward."

Boy Solo: Dirty faced steel mill worker (red work hankie) mopping forehead, talking to himself, counting money in pocketbook. "I ain't got 'nuff."

All: Sixteen Tons

All: Leven Cent Steel

Quotation: Under a spreading chestnut tree
          The village smithy stands,
          The smith, a mighty man is he,
          With strong and sinewy hands,
          And the muscles of his brawny arms
          Are strong as iron bands!

All: The Blacksmith Sings Merrily (as someone pounds shoe on anvil)

All: The Blacksmith

4.

Girl Solo: And thus the story goes
          From trading post we got Chicago Town.

Girl Solo: Our numbers grew by the score
          As thousands of immigrants found rest on our shore.

Low: Steel hoofs blazed the long trail down . . .

Middle: East was linked to west by rail . . .

High: From 13 colonies to the great 48

All: Linked together by rails of steel
          One nation indivisible!

Girl Solo: We grew! We grew! We grew!

Solo: And man forged his steel as on we grew . . .

Low: And sang his working song . . .

All: Drill Ye Tarriers!

Girl Solo: Man has always dreamed . . .
          He worked, and as he worked he dreamed.

Low: He dreamed that he could fly . . .

Middle: He dreamed, yes dreamed, yes dreamed!

High: He dreamed that he could fly!

5.

All: And so on wings of steel—he flew, he flew, he flew!

Girl Solo: This wonderful story of the growth of steel

Could never have been possible
Could never have been real . . .
Girl Solo: Without, without, without . . .
Low: The unity of purpose . . .
Middle: The zeal, the zeal, the zeal.
High: Of all the people working together!
with everybody's shoulder to the wheel!
All: It Takes Everybody to Build This Land.

WE MAKE CHOICES

Making choices is part of the democratic way of life. Too many children are never permitted to make choices, however, and thus never learn the important lesson inherent in having made a poor one.

In all creative expression the child has a series of choices to make. The first one is what medium is to be used to express his idea. Words, clay, paint, rhythm, melody—all are possibilities. His idea springs from his experiences. Out of his stockpile of experiences, therefore, he selects the one idea with which he wishes to work—his second choice. He discovers that he may need to gather more data or do some experimenting; after he is satisfied with his findings he is ready to organize and record. His idea may flower in any form but he is committed to some sort of product. Time and again in the process he has sorted and chosen and rejected. From the very beginning when he decided to write a poem, story, or play he had something to say—his choices had to do with *how.*

His next choice, and it must be his own, will be with whom he wishes to share what he has created. His right not to share at all must be respected by the adult. His right to show it only to an adult in whose integrity he has absolute confidence should also be respected. Products children are proud of they usually wish to bring to their peer group. On the other hand, sometimes when they write about their fears, angers, frustrations, hates they may wish to keep them to themselves.

There will be times when children write stories that are crude and vulgar. (This does not refer to colorful slang or colloquial language, but rather to profane and obscene expressions.) Sometimes the language they use is the only language they know to express deep-seated feelings. Sometimes it is done to try out the teacher—to see if he really means that they may write as they will. Occasionally it is done just to be smart. When such writing occurs it may be necessary to discuss with the child his motives, to explain that while his language is picturesque it is not appropriate in school and that although there is no rule against writing as he must or wishes, it cannot be shared. If the child knows no other words, you can help him find substitute expressions; those trying you out or the smart talkers may find the pressure for peer group acceptance stronger than the urge to continue as they are doing without the opportunity to share.

Usually, and rightly so, the first sharing is on the oral-aural level. As the children tell or read their creations, they are hearing themselves say what they think. This speaking of their material is often more significant in the child's written expression than a perfectly written copy. Sometimes you, if the child wishes, may read the materials in order that the full beauty or force of the product may be savored.

Another choice that the child has to make concerns proofreading, correcting, and rewriting. Some teachers have found it good to operate on the principle that if the child wants to share his product in written form, it should be put into acceptable correct form for the reader. Thus a child may decide that as far as he is concerned it is finished. He has written it or told it, and this is the end. If there is a rough copy, it is dropped in a folder. On the other hand, if he wants to take it home, put it on the bulletin board, or submit it to the school newspaper, he must accept the discipline of proofreading and correction. All the help that he needs should be given him in this event, but the responsibility is his. A child may be discouraged from future creative writing if everything he writes must be rewritten. Many children are more eager to go to new ideas for stories and poems than to rework old ones. If we believe that the process is more important than the product, then we will let the child be the judge of where to place his efforts.

THE COURT WILL COME TO ORDER

The way each day is lived is a judgment of the effectiveness of the days that have preceded it. Why then make of evaluation a fetish, a thing apart, a fearsome rite? Here separated from the teaching of skills and facts, here on this little island set apart from the conformities of everyday living, here where we are concerned with ideas and what children do with them— here, do we care to suspend judgment? Can we gratefully accept the periods, commas, quotation marks and correctly spelled words that find their way into their writing? Do we dare to ignore these except when they must be there for the sake of clarity? Do we dare to say that Johnny has grown in turning a phrase, in interpreting a character, in describing a feeling, in accepting other children's criticism while defending his own uniqueness, in expressing himself succinctly, in organizing ideas into a satisfying sequence?

Creating does not take place all of the time. This happens just some of the time. This is a brief period set aside in a busy workaday world for creating for fun, for promoting good mental health, for developing aesthetically, for organizing what we know, and for better understanding ourselves and others.

Is it good . . . is it bad? Who knows, or who is to say, except the creator? As adults it is difficult to withhold our judgments, to permit the creator to fumble and grope until he has found the pattern that satisfies him, the pattern that he knows is right for him. Some day, some year—after much maturing—he will ask for honest criticism, and at that time some experienced adult should be ready to advise him. How well qualified you—as elementary teachers—are to dabble in literary criticism I am loath to say. Most of the time, however, while the child is in the elementary school the help you give will be of a different kind. You should encourage him to talk out his ideas, to enrich his experiences, to gather data. You should ask questions that will encourage his thinking, but not make suggestions. Offering a word or a phrase is likely to make the child insecure in his own thinking and judgment. What he needs he will find deep within himself. Help him to draw up from the well of his subconscious what is his. Try not to superimpose on him your own idea. Yours may be a good idea for you but it is not his idea, and may be quite inappropriate for his stage of development. Let your spirit and enthusiasm and faith in him carry him forward to the point at which he can say "It is mine, and I approve of it."

A word of warning. Let us never forget that this attitude is appropriate only when the child is creating. Let us never forget that this small island will be ever circumscribed by speaking and writing experiences in which conventional correctness will be expected, even demanded. Can you keep "hands off" while he arranges language symbols in a creative way to make a poem, a story, or a play? You can and you will if you prize language that is unique and personal and a living thing.

Let them use language to cushion the shock of reality—a reality that is not always understandable but one that the eager youngsters seldom shirk, one that often hurts but must be explored. A driving pulsing urge to go forward into each new experience carries them toward a great unknown—maturity. They will solve their problems as they go along because today has been a good day, the very best preparation for tomorrow.

READING LIST

Applegate, Mauree. *Helping Children Write* (Evanston, Ill.: Row, Peterson and Co., 1954).

Arnstein, Flora J. *Adventure into Poetry* (Stanford, Calif.: Stanford University Press, 1953).

Burrows, Alvina T. *et al. They All Want to Write* (New York: Prentice-Hall, 1952).

Elementary English (Champaign, Ill.: National Council of Teachers of English).

Mearns, Hughes. *Creative Youth* (Garden City, New York: Doubleday, 1925).

3

You Can't Teach Art, Thank Goodness!

But, luckily, he kept his wits and his purple crayon.[1]

YOU ARE A TEACHER of children. You deal in the skills, knowledge, and attitudes that foster self-realization, human relationships, civic responsibility, and economic efficiency. You can't draw a man or a horse. Perhaps you have a supervisor who can teach children how to draw and how to paint. This is beside the point, however. You are responsible for children's growth and development, and art expression is a channel that needs to be kept open and free of obstruction.

Even without materials the very young child finds tools and surfaces to use for drawing. He uses his fingers, his hands, even his elbows and feet. He uses sticks, shells, stones or any other sharp instrument that comes to hand. Lacking paper he draws on walls, floors, windows, sidewalks, or in mud, gravel, or sand. He models with mud, dough, or any other malleable material that he finds. When he is young he is ingenious. Often his very ingenuity gets him into trouble, and if alternate materials are not provided and too much punishment occurs he is apt to develop a distaste for all art expression.

[1] Crockett Johnson, *Harold and His Purple Crayon* (New York: Harper and Bros., 1955), (unnumbered).

WHAT IS YOUR ROLE IN THE PROPER DEVELOPMENT
OF MENTAL AND CREATIVE GROWTH?

Not teaching but helping children unfold through the use of a wide variety of media—paint, paper sculpture, crayons, clay, sewing, finger paint, collage, and others—is your privilege. Art expression, like physical maturation, develops from the inside to the outside, if the adults in the child's life space provide a good climate, fertile soil, sunshine and rain. This is an atmosphere in which respect, love, and understanding abound. Here no plant is turned back to "do it over . . . make another flower because this one is a runt or the wrong color or too this or too that." Nature never painted two autumn leaves the same or frosted the window glass with somebody else's pattern. You can help the children to find the limits of their media, you can agree on the standards for cleaning up, you can provide materials of all kinds—but you can't tell or show them how or what to draw. You can teach them to hold a brush, to mix paint, to knead clay, to manage a pair of scissors or a knife or other tools, but the subject matter of the individual must come from the individual.

The subject matter for his composition will grow out of his experiences, real and vicarious. You have an important part to play here. You not only see that he constantly has ever-widening experiences, but in addition to this, you also help him to discover the importance of what happens to him as subject matter for his creations. His reactions to, feelings about, concern for—all find their way into his media of expression. In these activities you make no judgments. You are the catalyst that encourages the fusion of the individual, his experience, and his expression. The individual himself must grope with his media until he has said what he has meant to say, in the way that he wants to say it, and he must be the sole judge of the point at which he can approve of it. When he is older, and real artistic talent is evident, then and then only will he need the professional help of an artist. We have no right to say that this is good or bad, right or wrong when a child is groping to express an idea; and furthermore, who are we to evaluate in a field in which we are untutored and alien? You like Picasso, I like Grant Wood. Does this make me a critic of art? Some of our pet ideas of horizon lines, proportion, and perspective are completely ignored by many famous artists. When children use art as a means of self-expression, these concepts should not be taught by elementary teachers. Your job of teaching in this area is of a different kind.

In the graphic and three-dimensional arts, as in the other areas of creativity, the values themselves do not vary. We see free personal expression as having aesthetic, therapeutic, and social significance, with the additional value found in the pleasure of doing and creative critical thinking.

We recognize here, as well as in other areas, that all children cannot share their own unique ideas with paint, crayons, or clay. Some will express themselves with words, some with their bodies, and only some with art media. It is important that all should have the opportunity to experiment with these media, "scribble" if you like, but eventually they must be given the opportunity to make their own choices of media.

Furthermore, let it be remembered that there is a need for both appreciating and producing. Criteria to measure a child's own work are developed by becoming familiar with the works of the masters as well as of his peer group. No artist should leave him with feelings of inferiority and inadequacy. Each artist should be studied in terms of uniqueness. So, too, in studying the works of his peer group and other children there should be no adverse comparison, but rather a careful appraisal of the individuality of each contribution. From these aesthetic experiences in appreciation, the child establishes his criteria for judging what syndrome of qualities contributes to making art understandable.

In order to show how a child unfolds in artistic personal expression, the writer would like to summarize, in simple terms, the developmental levels as described by Viktor Lowenfeld.[2] This is not for the art student or art education major, but rather for that army of classroom teachers who are expected to direct a program of free creative expression without special training in the various aesthetic fields. Art, music, and dance

[2] Viktor Lowenfeld, *Creative and Mental Growth* (New York: The Macmillan Co., 1952).

consultants can help us to understand the process, can provide materials, and can teach skills; but for those of us who have no special teachers or consultants there are certain basic understandings that may help.

THE SCRIBBLER

As the child shows a disposition for holding a pencil or a crayon, if his activity is not interfered with, he is most likely to practice (drill himself) in disorderly scribbling. At this level he is not consciously thinking about what is on the paper, but rather he is growing in muscular control. Sometime later he begins to realize that there is a relationship between his hand, the crayon, and the paper. He finds himself repeating the same motion over and over again, and he sees himself producing lines which are similar. With the recognition that he can control the crayon, he swings around and produces circular forms and also swinging horizontal or vertical lines that move up and down or across and back. Now he begins to be aware of the fact that his mind is controlling his hand. He can make the crayon do again a thing that he has found good. He begins to combine longitudinal and circular scribble. This is often the beginning of the drawing of a man. Shortly after this he crosses a real Rubicon. He begins to name his scribble. There is no attempt at making the lines look like what he calls them, but he is composing a story, a web woven from the threads of his own experiences. He is using symbols to represent the familiar things, people, and activities in his environment. He is using his thinking and his motor skill to make a record of something that is important to him. With his scribble, the child tells us his story. Without his verbalizing we do not understand what he is saying, but he is on his way.

Most children are long past the scribble stage when they come to school, but there are those who are squarely in the middle of it. There are also those whose scribbling has been so seriously interfered with that it is necessary for the kindergarten or first-grade teacher to help the child find his way back to a new beginning. Sometimes, if the child is inflexible with one medium—such as crayons, a change to paint, plasticine or clay may help him to find his base in pure manipulation and move through the other stages toward the next level. A child can scribble with many materials. In fact, it seems to the writer that with each new material the child should be encouraged to scribble until he has some control of that medium. Scribbling may be compared with the babbling of the baby before he produces conventional verbal symbols, or with the kicking, waving of arms and legs, and other random physical movements before he crawls, sits, stands, and walks deliberately. With each new medium of expression he needs to discover its limits and possibilities. Fumbling around and trying out may have a salutary effect upon his later efforts.

Children will vary greatly as to the length of time they stay in these stages of the scribble level, but ultimately they will move into what Lowenfeld calls the preschematic stage and Mendelowitz terms the search for a symbol.

THE SEARCH BEGINS

In searching for a symbol the child constantly changes his form until he finds what he judges to be right for him. Early in this stage he draws into his forms only those parts that are important to him at the time. Thus he may draw a head, two arms and two legs—or only a head and two arms. Subconsciously he knows that he and the people in his world have other features and parts, but until they are needed for some function in his drawing or until he is sensitized to the function they serve they will be omitted. Each detail that he adds to his emerging schema is a step toward intellectual maturity. It is not suggested that teachers tell children to add parts, but rather to bring them to the threshold of consciousness by experiences that pin-point their presence or function. Thus, when children consistently omit ears, fingers or other body parts, a sensory experience of listening for something or modeling clay, with discussion accompanying the activity about what it feels like and then drawing themselves involved in these activities may bring the omitted parts into their schemas.

In this stage the child is unaware of spatial relationships. Those spatial relationships that he does show are usually emotional ones. Objects will be placed in no special or logical arrangement on his paper. As in the early stages of picture interpretation, he draws "Here is a house, here is a car, here I am—I am holding my rabbit."

His colors at this stage are chosen because he likes them, and he makes little effort to relate them to reality unless adults have told him to do so. Again, as with spatial relationships, chosen colors may approach the realistic when there is a strong emotional attachment to the object. Thus a beloved green tractor may be proudly painted green and, as a matter of fact, all tractors may be green to him. His colors are chosen largely, however, because of personal appeal, and it is not unusual to find purple hair or yellow sky.

Fostering growth will always be in terms of sensory experiences which will lead him in the direction of his thinking. Imposing upon him standards that are inappropriate to his developmental stage—e.g., horizon lines or proportion—may interfere with his free expression. Usually, however, children will take only those steps for which they are ready.

OVER AND OVER AND OVER AGAIN

During the next phase of his creative growth, the child gradually arrives at his schema (symbols) for man drawing, proportion, spatial relationships, color and other elements of expression. He discovers that everything stands on something. He uses the edge of the paper or draws on a base line. The objects go marching across the paper one at a time with no overlapping. He discovers a blue sky above him, and almost without exception he puts at the top of his paper a strip of blue sky and usually a large yellow sun. The space in between is not filled in except for those things standing upright on the base line. He is not ready for the concept that earth and sky merge. To hurry him into this mode of expression is inappropriate for his developmental level. If he is aware of uneven terrain, his base line will move up and down with objects standing perpendicular to it—e.g., the chimney on the roof. If all of the objects in his story do not fit on the base line, he is apt to draw a second one with the objects or persons. He may portray several scenes in one drawing—leaving for school, going to school, and arriving at school.

When the straight-away base line does not serve the child's purpose, he may discover the fold-over or draw the base line around his paper. In the fold-over he either turns his paper upside-down or walks around it and draws another unit with its own base and sky. When folded on the base lines the objects stands face to face as on two sides of a street or river. In the continuous base line he may draw a four-sided figure like a baseball diamond with all players standing on the base facing in.

At the same time—as he experiments with the base line— he is likely to show the outside and the inside of a house, public building, cave or factory, etc. if the emotional experience is one in which exterior and interior are involved. This is called X-ray drawing.

As the child gropes his way around in space, he is also groping for his object symbols. He tries this and that, usually combining geometric forms of circles, rectangles, and straight lines. At this stage he almost completely ignores dress or other differentiation between male and female. It is quite likely that the more sensitive and alert he is, the more details he will include. When he finds a satisfying form for man or house or tree, he will draw it again and again. Basically it will remain the same, but in order to show a specific experience he may use omission, exaggeration, or change. These deviations from his schema usually result when the experience has been a highly emotional one. Thus if he is catching a ball, picking flowers, or hugging his dog his arms may be out of all proportion to the rest of his drawing. On the other hand, he may completely ignore some other body part that has no significance in this story.

Another area of schema is color. As stated previously, he discovers that the sky is blue. Rain, snow, or sleet in the composition usually will not change this. Often pictures will have a yellow sun shining right through the rain. Trees will be green and leafly even in a snowstorm. Grass will always be green.

My choice is clay — in my own way

Significant in this phase is the point at which the child begins to repeat the same symbol again and again. This usually means that he has found a schema of which he can approve, and through the repetition of it he finds security and satisfaction. He makes changes only as an emotional impact dictates change.

There should be no attempt made to hurry children through these stages. Moving at their own rate through the various phases, groping toward their ultimate discovery, stopping to reinforce what they have learned, and finally moving on—they are thus most likely to be stable, healthy personalities, able to meet problems and solve them to their own satisfaction.

IT MUST LOOK REAL

As in all developmental tasks, children vary greatly in the length of time they stay in any one phase. After an individually determined amount of schematic repetition the child moves on again—this time into a stage of realism. Simultaneously he enters the gang age. During this period the youngster's major characteristic is one of conformity to peer group standards. When group standards and adult standards differ he is often unco-operative with older people. Adults responsible for him— teachers and parents specifically—may find him quite negative to their suggestions and demands. Now, as much as at any time in his life, the child needs the support of adults who understand his conflicts and problems.

It is quite likely that much of the free-wheeling thinking, large swinging movements, free action-packed art of the last phase will disappear. Symbols become stiff, costumes assume great importance, male and female roles have significance, and the child's ability to please himself is almost nonexistent. During this period the child may find his satisfaction in crafts, since often with these materials he is more nearly able to meet the test of realism. Only the unusual child can withstand the pressures of conformity at this age. Carried with the tide of this preadolescent crisis, the teacher or parent watches so much that was beautiful pass away, to return for only a few after the crisis has passed. Our job is one of keeping the gates open, of providing materials, and of constantly valuing the unique, the original, the creative. Creativity may all but take a holiday, but the gates must be kept open for its return.

The preadolescent attempts to draw, paint, or model realistically. He often uses his time to create designs for clothing, furniture, or drapes. He discovers the plane, and the sky comes down to meet the earth. Working in a group he discovers the need for overlapping, with one object partially obscuring another. As individuals work together with cut paper or collage materials they develop group relationships.

In figure drawing preadolescents omit almost completely the earlier geometric shapes and drop their schema. As they dress the figures in costumes, uniforms, female and male clothing, carefully drawing in hair, eyebrows, fingernails and the like, they are trying to make the symbol as realistic as possible.

Knowing these phases of normal development alerts the teacher to changing moods, methods, and materials. Her efforts will be devoted to maintaining a healthy creative environment in which the child feels his freedom to think for himself, to solve his own problems, to make his own judgments.

GUIDING ACTIVITIES

In the kindergarten and primary grades you should provide boxes of scrap material (collage), crayons, thick water paint, plasticine, clay, colored construction paper. You should see that children have time to savor their personal experiences. You should be sure that they—as groups and as individuals—have time to express what they know, feel, see, and imagine in an art media, as well as time to evaluate their efforts in terms of their own criteria.

It is possible to do these things within the limits of your busy day. It is possible because you value children's free uninhibited expression. It is possible because you believe in children and in their inherent goodness. It is possible because you are wise enough to know that there are preliminary steps to go through in order for these young children to develop self-discipline and control. In establishing a code of behavior, the rights and privileges of the individuals become evident. It is only after these rights and privileges are clearly understood by the children that the teacher can go about her business of helping this group or that child develop skills, learn facts, gain appreciations while others use art media for personal self-expression.

Long before you turn children loose to pursue their own interests, you have shared with them art of both the masters and comparable age groups. You have talked about the importance of being oneself, of digging deep within to find ways of drawing, modeling, or arranging ideas. You have discussed the fact that copying other people's ideas is unworthy. You have discussed the idea that each child will not necessarily choose art media to record his ideas, but that each is welcome to experiment with various media and to gain control over them; if, however, he finally turns away from these activities for other creative outlets, no one will think the less of him.

A CODE TO LIVE BY

Standards for using materials should be established. The importance of living by this code cannot be overemphasized. Dirty paint brushes, spilled paint, uncovered clay pots and droppings of clay, untidy floors, tools not returned to their proper places—these mean that others' rights are being interfered with. Rules imposed by teachers or a mere verbal rehearsal of what the child thinks the teacher wants him to say simply won't work. The involvement of children in setting up a code in which they can see sense, the lettering of that code on a chart and placing it in work and material centers puts the responsibility squarely on them for their own and peer group cooperation. The teacher will always be the final authority, and will need from time to time to withdraw privileges from those children who have not learned how to handle freedom. Other children's rights need to be protected from those who cannot conform. Important as this discipline is, it must not become a stumbling block to creative expression, and the insightful teacher will know when to temper justice with need.

ON THEY GO

Planning should be done at the beginning of the day, evaluating at the end. Talking it over? Is this not already a part of your daily program? So without taking time from any other activity in your busy day, you can include creative opportunities. Instead of doing all the busy work, the seat work that you have spent so much time on, children are learning to use their time advantageously. Drillwork as needed should continue, but as children choose creative activities and carry them out, you are freed from much of the entertaining or keeping children busy and can devote your time to teaching small groups at their developmental levels. Nothing in your classroom is changed really except the use by children of their free time, of which there is often so much in a child's school day. This free time may be used by all the children for art projects. Children may also be writing, dramatizing, singing, dancing, and constructing.

In the middle grades children need to continue the free expression of the preschematic and schematic stages. Changes will occur, but the supporting atmosphere, the provision of materials, and time to create are still of primary importance. As these youngsters sense a stronger need to conform, their art is likely to lose the qualities of free-swinging bigness and stiffness will appear; but this, although you may often deplore it, is to be expected, and you should not attempt to hold children back at a less mature level. Given generous sympathetic adults who understand the growth process, those children who have an inclination toward art activities as an emotional and aesthetic outlet will find their way back to originality.

READING LIST

Lindstrom, Miriam. *Children's Art* (Berkeley, Calif.: University of California, 1957).

Lowenfeld, Viktor. *Creative and Mental Growth* (New York: The Macmillan Co., 1952).

———. *Your Child and His Art* (New York: The Macmillan Co., 1954).

Mendelowitz, Daniel M. *Children Are Artists* (Stanford, Calif.: Stanford University Press, 1953).

School Arts. Stanford University, California.

4

I Am My Own Instrument

There was nothing
but the beat of his own heart
to establish his rhythm.

With a slow lethargic motion
he glided across the floor.

Fear entered, pulse accelerated,
feet carried him—pound, pound, pound—
away from the fear stimuli.

He gasped and sank to the floor.

Breathing became slower, slower, slower.

Only his chest and pulse record
the beat, beat, beat—a tom-tom in his head.

Now he starts up again—to his knees, one.

To his feet, two.

Neck up and forward, three.

Up go his arms, four.

And he moves out into space.

More quickly now his cautious steps
carry him from corner to corner.

Head motions say,
"Nothing here, or here, or here."

Faster and faster he whirls
into a veritable swirling dervish of motion.

Ecstasy flows from his body.

Higher and higher he leaps and soars.

44

> With a cry of exaltation
> he swings high into space.
> Suspended in air for that breathless moment,
> then down, down, down.
> Knees, trunk, head, arms, prone at last.
> Muscles quiver and still.
> A gush of expelled air;
> complete release;
> a soft sigh;
> eyelids close.

Without a single word the dancer had told his story. From the depths of his subconscious he had brought his fears to the threshold and found them only figments of his imagination.

To the "beat beat beat of the tom-tom" life is rhythm. From the birth cry to the last gasp, life is rhythm. In time with the universe or in contradiction to it, life is rhythm. Patterns are found within and are superimposed from without. Flowing, pulsing, pushing, pulling. You can set the stage to free the spirit.

> Rhythm is something we share in common, you and I, with all the plants and animals and peoples in the world, and with the stars and moon and sun and all the whole vast wonderful universe beyond this wonderful earth which is our home.[1]

THERE ARE NO RULES

Children dance as naturally as they breathe. The heart is a built-in metronome which, as it propels the life-stream through arteries and veins, beats out its pulsing rhythm. The muscles establish another, as does the central nervous system. In time with the swaying wheat, the surging tide, the shifting sand, the cyclic planting and reaping, the alternating days and nights, the changing seasons, the human child moves and grows.

What then makes teachers reluctant to encourage children to try an outlet as natural as breathing? With young children there

[1] Langston Hughes, *The First Book of Rhythms* (New York: Franklin Watts, Inc., 1954), p. 63.

are no rules to be learned, no skills to be taught, no routines to be followed, no demonstrations to be given. Formal dance steps and the choreographer's patterns have no place in the ordinary classroom in the elementary school.

As in other media, the talented or gifted children eventually yearn for more formal teaching—for the external discipline found in the scales in music, the basic steps and positions in ballet, the mechanics of writing, and anatomy in art. But this comes much later and only for those who ask to be taught, ask to be shown.

Creative rhythm in the elementary school is just another means of expression, of communication, of sharing ideas. Expression to bring the personal satisfaction that the child derives from the act, or to tell a story to someone else. It is expression that relieves inner tension or explodes into a new symbol of past experiences. Expression that may be a paean of joy or a cry of sorrow.

I CAN'T DANCE

Can you sit still when you hear the martial music of a marching band? Do you sway gently to Brahms' *Lullaby*? Are you not gliding inside to the *Skater's Waltz* and tap-tap-tapping to a fox trot or a schottische? Have you never in the privacy of your own room let yourself go? Completely abandoning your inhibitions, have you never whirled and glided, stomped and swung? Or even though you have never actually done so, surely you have *felt* like letting yourself go. Great exaltation must, at some time, have made you feel as though you could fly. So, your body is your prison. It wasn't always true, and it need not be for these youngsters whose lives you touch today.

IT'S NOT WHAT YOU DO, BUT HOW YOU FEEL

You should start with yourself. No, I don't mean you must dance. Fine if you care to but it isn't necessary, and certainly if you're practicing so you can teach it—it's better that you *don't* know how. Let the children show you. Let them show how much you value their uniqueness. Let them feel your support in every one of their little personal motions that is not stiffly reproduced from dancing school patterns and TV stereotypes. Resist the temptation to comment negatively on copied movements, and warmly applaud genuine attempts to let the body tell its story. Honestly and forthrightly admire the things that children do, these movements that the years and stultifying experiences prevent you from doing. Let your feelings show through in the gladness in your eyes and the smile on your face. This is not "Isn't he cute?" but rather "How beautifully Johnny's body swings the scythe."

Perhaps the very fact that fewer of us have tried this creative activity than any other gives us an advantage. The temptation to show people *how* certainly grows out of our own successful experiences, so without this experience perhaps it will be easier to say, "I don't know how to do it . . . I don't know how you feel . . . how do you think it should be done?" Since there is no right or wrong, since there is no rule of thumb, since this must evolve from the body centers and move along the nerve and muscle fibers, since this is something that nobody except the creator can feel—what do you have to lose?

Your children, at least when you first meet them in school, have seldom developed self-consciousness. Fortunate indeed are those children whose teachers, like you, will encourage them to continue to use their bodies throughout childhood and later years to tell stories, illustrate a mood, or simply enjoy the feeling of well-being that derives from rhythmic movements.

MY INSTRUMENT IS ME

Tapping feet,
Nodding heads,
Clapping hands,
Swaying backs,
Shrugging shoulders
        and
Walking, running, hopping,

Skipping, leaping, jumping,
Swinging, bending, stretching,
Galloping, cantering, bounding,
Pulling, punching, twisting,
Shaking, beating, splashing.

The body and body parts weave the various motions into a simple or complex design. As the rhythmic pattern evolves, drums, tom-toms, castanets, and rattles can pick up and follow the beat. Music newly created or matched to the rhythm can accompany the dancer. If you can play an instrument, good. If not, use records or beat a drum. Other children too are often skillful helpers. The creative act itself, however, is the individual's. Although sometimes children's dance routines are combined into larger units, each routine is individually created. Often as not the activity should begin and end as a one-man act. There will, of course, be times when children enjoy learning another child's dance, and in turn the creator will enjoy teaching others. Circumstances will dictate how and when this is to be done.

I DON'T KNOW WHERE TO START

No, of course you don't — you are hesitant about the first step. You are afraid the children may get out of hand if allowed too much liberty. But all this time you have been working with them toward self-control, self-discipline, self-direction. Each and every creative activity has as its most cherished goal self-control. Why worry then? Face up to the fact—especially if the youngsters have already had their attitudes colored by the idea that dancing is a "sissy" business—that there may be some silliness, some horseplay, some plain boisterousness. When they act the clown, remember that clowning can be rhythmical, that horseplay is a highly skilled and remunerative activity. Start where they are. The comedy dancer is not a social outcast. If they want to clown, let them. They want to act the "fool." Good. Let them act in rhythmical patterns that give the children a sense of accomplishment and pride.

Our bodies tell our stories well

DRAMATIZING LIFE AND STORIES

Using daily life experiences, young children can dance everything from washing dishes, doing the laundry, and mowing the
lawn to painting the house and shingling the roof. As they start
to move rhythmically, sometimes for solo dancing, sometimes
with the leader setting the pattern and others following, they
lose themselves in a world of make-believe. Home, school, and
neighborhood routines are played out in rhythm by lone dancers
or teams while other children beat time or strum chords in
accompaniment: leaves falling, flowers unfolding, horses pranc-
ing, elephants plodding, trains rushing, planes soaring, boats
sailing. The yakity-yakity-yak of the current gun hero, the clomp-
clomp-clomp of the horses' hooves, or the drip-drip-drip of the
rain may stir the blood and set the pulses throbbing. The
dancers should be encouraged to do it in their own way and

according to their own design, and some will—if you manage to keep hands off.

Later the children may dance fairy and folk tales, realistic stories of the here-and-now and of the long-ago and far-away. Without verbal interpretation of any kind in their own ballet, they carry the plot with body movements. We have seen children dance *The Three Little Pigs* and *Hansel and Gretel*, chapters from *Homer Price, Huckleberry Finn,* and the *Landing of the Pilgrims*. How to do it? Let the children show you. They have so many more resources for imagining than most adults. Planning how to portray a story through dancing has value in that it is a creative process in itself.

INTERPRETIVE MOOD RHYTHMS

At the beginning of this chapter a boy dancing a fear mood was described. Joy, sorrow, wonder, enchantment, and despair can be and are expressed by body movements. To "show how" is not important, but to be able to recognize the child's attempts for *what he means them to be* is essential. "Make your body show how you feel" is better than "Why don't you do it this way?" The first snow may set them off in a happy mood, as may tomorrow's picnic or the day before Christmas. A beloved pet dies or a friend moves away, and unhappy feelings may result. Bringing these happy or unhappy feelings to the surface through body movement can help some children face reality. Never expect all children to use the dance—nor any other outlet —for emotional release, but encourage children who seem to profit from rhythms to try out their feelings in this way. Words, sounds, colors often can be beautifully expressed in rhythmic movements. This form of dancing will most often be of a solo type, and a corner of the room where a few can experiment (screened perhaps from other children involved in other enterprises) may produce breath-takingly lovely results.

SPORTS AND GAMES, TOO

In the middle grades when gangs are the cultural pattern, group rhythms are especially satisfying. Don't try to find ideas in this or any other book, but rather let the impetus spring from its natural source—the young, vibrant person. It is often more difficult to stop ideas, once they start to flow, than to find them. Seasonal sports are a never-ending source of rhythmic patterns. The wind-up, the pitch, the strike, the catch. Fielding and running and a dance is begun. A rainy day baseball game—what fun! Tackling and punting, running and passing. Relays and shot put, high jump and hurdles. Archery and tennis, swimming and boating. The appeal of these sports to most boys is universal. Not only are these activities satisfying in themselves, but often as the preadolescent gains control over his body his timing in the real sport will improve. Movement, when the impulse flows from the body centers rather than from some external command, seems to call forth a natural fluidity and grace.

Girls, too, will find themes in rope jumping, skating, hoop rolling, baton twirling, and in many of the same sports that the boys enjoy. There is scarcely a human or animal activity that cannot be cast into rhythm.

Why bother, you may ask, to take ideas from all these sources? Why not the actual sport? These rhythms do not substitute for but rather correlate with the real thing. However there are activities that children may get the feel of long before they engage in them as competitive sports.

The boys and girls will think of many other games not listed here, and it will be better to let them lead the way.

If from the beginning they are encouraged to use the dance to express ideas they create original square and folk dances, too. Rhythms provide just another sensory channel for organizing what they know and feel into some sort of visible expression. Using imagination and logical thinking, they will pour out fresh viewpoints and unique sequences that will be pleasurable and satisfying to themselves and to others.

IS IT GOOD? IS IT BAD?

Well, at least you don't have to mark a creative activity "A" or "B". You aren't a judge. It is lovely, or it is graceful, or it expresses exactly what the child is attempting to portray, it may be that the strong beat of the Indian War Dance is reproduced very clearly. But these are your reactions, based on your criteria, and as such they are quite unimportant. What *is* important is "Does the creator feel refreshed, relaxed, unwound, cleansed, healed, fatigued but happy?" The child says: "That *was* fun. I felt like I was a plane flying, or a flower growing and blooming, or a leaf falling, or a river flowing. I was what I always wanted to be, and it was a good feeling."

For each and every child whom you help to find the freedom to let his muscles and mind take over his wonderful rhythmic life pattern you can give yourself a plus mark. Give him an accepting climate, space to fly, encouragement to try—and you have earned your "A."

READING LIST

Andrews, Gladys. *Creative Rhythmic Movement for Children* (Englewood Cliffs, N. J.: Prentice-Hall, Inc., 1954).

Childhood Education (Washington, D.C.: Association for Childhood Education International).

Cole, Natalie Robinson. *The Arts in the Classroom* (New York: The John Day Co., 1940).

Hughes, Langston. *The First Book of Rhythms* (New York: Franklin Watts, Inc., 1954).

5

My Heart Sings Its Own Melody

VIRGINIA AUSTIN

WHAT IS MUSICAL CREATIVITY?

ANY SITUATION in which the learner must depend upon and draw from *himself*, his past experiences, his present knowledge and skill, as a means of expressing his own personal ideas or emotions through a musical medium can be called a musically creative situation. He does not get the music or the emotion from a book or from another person or from some other source outside himself, but from within himself.

The final musical product in which this idea or emotion takes shape may not have very great merit in itself, especially if it is a first effort, but this product can be improved and refined. What *is* valuable to the learner is the internal reorganization and reworking and application of material that was necessary to evolve the product—a sort of digestion and invigoration.

For example, we are almost certain to find better songs in any song book than those a second- or sixth- grader makes up. But in the process—the *act* of creating a song, especially if he attempts to notate it—he will have to look into many musical matters and regulations, and is more likely to learn and retain with real understanding and insight much basic musical knowledge because it derives from his personal experience.

Thus, as a child creates a song he learns that poetry and music are closely related through meter, nuance, and inflection; that certain simple forms and patterns are used most commonly; that careful music notation (the correct use of clefs, key and measure signatures, notes and stems, sharps and flats, etc.) is essential if his song is to be recorded as he sang or played it.

By some medium of arts or crafts he can further enhance his song. If he complements his song with an oil or finger painting, a clay model or a charcoal drawing for example, he will discover how art—like music—is another means to express a mood, tell a story, clarify a text, enrich self-expression, or release tensions.

Manufactured instruments are almost certain to last longer and make a better sound than those that children make, but in the *act* of building an instrument a learner can come to understand more about sound—how it is made and where it comes from; the principle of a vibrating body and a resonating chamber; how pitch is changed by length or thickness or texture; what creates timbre, and so on. There is also the very practical result, of course, of gaining some usable rhythm and melody instruments.

THE VALUE OF CREATIVE LEARNING

We must keep in mind that one of the most important benefits of creativity is that it provides a means of utilizing information and skills in a functional and meaningful way. The learner has to make use of his skills and information so that they make sense and work, so that they are useful and productive. It provides a learning situation, an opportunity to learn from experience. Moreover, it is *not* experience which is directed *at* him or planned *for* him by others, but experience that is motivated, planned, provided, engineered and carried out by himself. It is the *learner* who decides how to use these skills, who carries out the work, who interprets the results. The product itself is secondary, however—more important is what happened to the learner in the process.

It is also a secondary and rather coincidental by-product to uncover a superior creative talent, because such a talent will find its way to creativity anyway. What is important is how the learner is changed and how he grows; the insights he acquires, musical and others; the attitudes he develops; the feelings he can bring to fruition and expression; the way his relationships to others bloom.

THE PERSON IS IMPORTANT

In a creative situation, the learner is the central motivating force rather than a leader or teacher or something outside himself. Thus it follows that interest is strongest, for need is present —a reason for being, for doing. The *climate for learning and growing* is at its best. The learner cares more because some of himself has gone into the process and the product. We might then define creativity as a sort of reutilization or reapplication of past experiences in the light of *personal interests and needs*.

Creativity provides an accepted channel for the outlets of emotions that are often difficult to express in another way. Especially effective is music, which has a direct line to the soul and spirit, so to speak. For example, a child nursing pent-up anger or frustration can stamp or pound his way through a warrior dance without censure, or beat out an original rhythm on a drum, or hammer and pound on soda bottle tops made into a crude shaker. A child feeling disappointed or rejected can dance it out to appropriate mood music, or dramatize the part of a Cinderella, or make up a song about a broken doll or a gloomy day, or finger paint with somber colors to suitable music. Children often express their joy and excitement about a forthcoming trip or celebration through spontaneous singing and dancing. Make-believe mothers lull their dolls to sleep, crooning their own lullabies. Two small girls compose a welcome-home song for Daddy; another pair produce a complete musical play, though no special occasion inspired it.

THE CLIMATE FOR CREATING

The teacher's attitude sets the tone. Demonstrate a willing and uncritical acceptance of any pupil's contribution wherever possible. Try to find some use for it, some value in it. Thus you use the can to make a drum even if it won't be a very good one; you use the phrase hummed even if it is not very suitable; you accept a child's version of a dance step even if it doesn't match the music too well; you remember that the lines of a poem don't have to rhyme, but if pupils are used to thinking in rhymed couplets you save unusual forms for later.

There are many classic situations where it is dangerous to make a mistake, or when it incurs displeasure, disapproval, or disgrace, and sometimes rightly so. All the more reason for us to encourage as many learning situations as possible where the free relaxed atmosphere of experimentation can be fostered. To make a mistake is part of being creative. A class held in tight rein has difficulty because the children are so afraid of being wrong that they will not try. Here the teacher must patiently and sympathetically establish a *climate for creating*.

Thus if the class is too inhibited or intimidated to venture forth with ideas, the teacher can begin to involve them by confronting them with choices: "We could use this word or that one—which do you like?" "We could make the tune go this way or that way—which do you think suits best?" (Later on, also ask why.) "Which sounds better in this paper cup shaker—rice or these pebbles?" "Which goes better—this step or that one?"

Once choices are ventured, then ideas begin to flow. The group sees that the teacher's attitude is democratic, that she considers their ideas seriously and with respect, that she does not insist on her own ideas or attempt to change what the class members offer, that it is not dangerous to make a mistake or humiliating to have one's own idea rejected for another's.

WHAT WE CAN LEARN

Beginning students may have been looking at music for weeks, beating rhythms, singing melodies, spelling scales, fingering strings or keys, striking bells or strumming chords. But when they write their own scores for rhythm band, for instance, they must observe more closely how to write a trill for a triangle; how the conductor knows what each player should be playing; why rests are as important as notes; how important a tiny dot may be; why careless music notation interferes with music reading; why a noisy instrument like a cymbal is used for occasional effect, like strong seasoning in food; how an ink smear can come to be "played" as part of the music!

It is the same with an advanced student of counterpoint, to give an example beyond the training of the nonmusician readers of this book, but which may demonstrate this point: on all levels of learning, creative experimentation fosters research which in turn promotes learning. When a student begins to write his own two-part Invention in the style of Bach, for instance, he must do careful research on the Inventions of Bach to understand more clearly how a theme enters and is imitated; the pattern of modulation; how a sequence is built; how to effect or avoid a cadence; how to build a stretto; how to achieve augmentation, inversion, and so on. Or when he arranges for string quartet he must inform himself about the range and limitations of each instrument, fingering problems, bowing techniques, and the like.

It is often found to be true that serious young composers are among the best informed musicians. In order to consolidate and express his own creative ideas, the young composer must understand what has gone before, and how and where his own ideas compare or differ.

FAN THE SPARK!

First attempts at musical creativity are the important ones, and every effort should be made to insure the success of these experiences. The teacher should not be discouraged by a first attempt that brings a faltering response from shy or wary pupils, but await the next opportunity to fan a spark. Though the first captured efforts be crude, a technique that often works is to accept such offerings with a matter-of-fact attitude that says plainly "Of course I knew you could do it all the time!" Then others find courage to add their own ideas and the class is off to its first success!

We are all familiar with the situation in which a child eagerly volunteers to act out or dramatize an idea, or demonstrate his idea for a dance step, and then stands foolishly doing nothing. He didn't have an idea to begin with, but just wanted to be the chosen one. How many times has the teacher sent such a child awkwardly back to his seat? How much better it would be if the teacher asked leading questions to help the child formulate an idea: "Should you be stiff or limp here?" "Do you want your face to smile or droop?" "Where will your tambourine fit in?" "How can you show that this music is in a hurry?"

Although we begin by encouraging and accepting any contribution, this does not mean that the musical product must *remain* on the level of the beginning efforts. Gradually the teacher suggests, helps polish and improve, broadens horizons. Even better, as children become familiar with the creative process and develop new insights and improved attitudes, they will begin to evaluate critically their own product even before the teacher makes a move to arouse self-criticism and build higher standards.

"This drum head is too loose," a child will say, "so we ought to make it tighter." "This flower pot (or spoon, or xylophone bar) is out of tune with the others. We ought to replace it." "The third line of our song is just like the first; why don't we change it?" "We ought to make the tune go down here to express the mood of gloom." "This chord is too monotonous. Why don't we try to vary it? This melody is too ordinary. Why can't we make it sound different?" "We keep using the same dance steps. Can't you show us a new one, or can't we work out a new one?"

There are those who feel that when a teacher interferes, criticizes, suggests, contributes, the experience is no longer "creative." But it is still creative if there is give-and-take between teacher and pupils, evaluation and discard, revision and critical analysis. It is through such an exchange between less skilled persons and the more skilled teacher that growth takes place. It is precisely as the result of the hesitancy to interfere with the class idea that standards stagnate and no growth takes place. The teacher is there to prod, raise questions, encourage comparisons, and stimulate evaluation.

READINESS FOR CREATING

Knowing when to interfere or to participate, and to what extent, requires a sensitive teacher. Here again the leader or teacher should keep in mind the goals of the group (and the goals she has for the group) and assist as little or as much as is necessary to achieve these goals. Being creative requires *some* background and foundation of experience. Beginners in *anything* do not have this, and the teacher will first have to provide this experience for her group. Just as there is a preparation period for reading—the reading readiness period—so there may have to be a period of readiness for creating.

Can a first-grader improvise a dance if he can't yet skip? Can a second-grader create his own melody if he can't carry a tune? Can a third-grader write his own poem if he has heard or read only a few? Can a fourth-grader make his own instrument —a tambourine, perhaps—if he has never played one? Can a fifth-grader improvise a simple descant or harmony part if he can't hold his own in part singing? Can a sixth-grader write his own musical show if he is still ignorant of note values, key signatures, and measure signatures? Can junior high schoolers create their own "folk-style" dances if they haven't danced a number of them? And so it goes. The answers and the solutions are obvious.

Sometimes readiness for and experiments in creating can go hand in hand. A beginner who has learned a tune employing the first five notes of his xylophone can be encouraged to re-arrange the five tones in a different order—his own idea—and perhaps to transfer them to another pitched instrument such as the piano, psaltery, meloharp, flower-pot-scale, etc. A novice on the flute can attempt to pick out tunes he knows or create his own with whatever tones he can blow. A newcomer to the autoharp can be encouraged to work out his own progression of chords, whether he has been taught any progressions yet or not. A beginner using drum sticks can be encouraged to improvise his own rhythm pattern using the strokes he has just learned.

In singing, there is no intervening tool or instrument, but

physically we are our very own musical instruments. The one qualification here is that some degree of mastery of the ability to carry a tune is required. For some, this is a process which takes time. It is probable that for beginners still struggling to learn to carry a tune, an atmosphere in which much creating is encouraged is the best assistance they could receive in their own vocal development.

Making musical instruments is a very tangible way to be creative. It is fun to transform cigar boxes, tin cans, rubber inner tubing, wood and sand paper, bamboo sticks, gourds, and other materials into drums, bongos, tambourines, shakers, sand blocks, triangles, claves, rhythm sticks, and the like. It is a means of almost sure success and quick achievement. A child cares more about these instruments because he made them, and he also knows more about how they work. Every classroom can have its rhythm orchestra, each child his choice of instrument. He becomes more aware of differences in musical sounds, more discriminating in his choices.

OUR AIMS

If a perceptive teacher knows what she is aiming for, the techniques come. What then would be our aims? From creative musical experiences the teacher would hope to have her pupils derive such values as the assimilation of new material; the beginnings of the techniques of simple research and critical analysis as aids to true learning; a growing understanding and appreciation of the beautiful, through knowledge and first-hand experience; and a blooming of the spirit.

HOW EVALUATE

To *evaluate* is harder. Here again, the emphasis should be on the learner more than on his product. Of course the teacher is glad to have assisted in uncovering a musical talent, a flair for poetry, a graceful dancer, a sharp ear, nimble fingers or toes. In such a case, the pupil should be encouraged to pursue further study and training.

But in the others, whose painting, dancing, improvising, composing, etc. will never progress beyond the realm of the amateur, the teacher will want to look at the persons themselves and measure how they have grown and changed. Have they progressed in developing attitudes of tolerance and experimentation, habits of comparison and analysis? Have they increased their ability to collaborate with others, to draw ideas from within themselves, to acquiesce to the choices of others? Have they acquired a keener ear for rhyme, phrase, meter and measure, musical line and shape? Have they gained clearer comprehension of musical notation, and an increasing familiarity with music of the masters, with poetry, literature and art of great talents and minds past and present? Have they become steeped in the music, art and letters of their own heritage? Have they shown evidence of a quickening response to beauty?

If these things are so, then the teacher can feel she has been successful. The child who is sensitive to beauty is richer all his life; and he whose heart can sing with his own melody carries his own beauty with him.

READING LIST

Bradley, Ruth O. *We Wrote a Symphony, So Can You!* (Boston: C. C. Birchard, 1952).

Coleman, Satis N. *Creative Music for Children* (New York: G. P. Putnam's Sons, 1922).

———. *Creative Music in the Home* (Valparaiso, Ind.: L. E. Myers and Co., 1928).

Fox, Lillian Mohr and L. Thomas Hopkins. *Creative School Music* (New York: Silver Burdett Co., 1936).

Krone, Beatrice Perham. *Music in the New School* (Chicago: Neil A. Kjos Music Co., 1941).

Music Educators Journal (Washington, D.C.: Music Educators National Conference).

Sheehy, Emma. *There's Music in Children* (New York: Henry Holt and Co., 1946).

6

Let's Go on Together

ALL CHILDREN HAVE GIFTS

A TREASURE HUNT has begun. A search for a channel or channels through which the child's uniqueness may emerge is under way. There is no act that cannot be performed in a personally characteristic way, no material that cannot be used creatively.

As children operate in their own society, they are constantly giving you, the teacher, clues about themselves. Watch carefully for those individual twists that suggest an activity or a material that just may be the child's "open sesame" to creativity. Some children's gifts seem to fairly leap at you from all directions. Other children's are so deeply buried in conforming behavior that they seem not to exist at all. But you can be sure that they do exist, and that your patience and encouragement can bring them forth. Capitalize on the clues they give you.

The hints may appear in a movement of the body, insight into number, a hummed tune, an apt remark, special feeling in drawing or modeling, dressing a doll, building with blocks, arranging the play corner, planning a play. Listing of activities in which they may be found could go on ad infinitum. Keep your eyes and ears and heart alert, for they are bound to appear sooner or later.

When you have caught a hint of a creative tendency exploit it—but subtly. Don't charge in with all throttles open or you may frighten it right back into obscurity. Carefully, painstakingly set the stage so that this talent may blossom in response to some stimulus—a magnet, pastels, a playhouse that needs decorating, scarves, an autoharp, bottles, a slide rule, a book, until you get that significant flash.

EACH CHILD IS UNIQUE

Oh yes, hair and eye color and size and weight and mental ability are unique to each child. You know all that. But he is also unique in his responses to stimuli, and it is often these stimuli that encourage the spark of genius or the flair of individuality. You can't call a class together and teach creative writing. You can't show children how to "make up" a dance or draw a picture. If the ideas are truly their own they may be ferreted out, but they can't be poured in as you would prime a well. When the tide is really running free each will be different. When children are free to express ideas in their own way there is no need to copy. They will rejoice in their own difference from others and they will genuinely applaud uniqueness in others. This attitude of pride in their own and joy in others' successes will develop as you prize what is truly their own.

How do you recognize a child's product as genuine? There is no recipe. As you learn the children better and better you will just know. Insight will deepen as their faith in themselves and your faith in them is constantly reaffirmed. Be generous. Give them the benefit of the doubt. If you are. not sure, then trust them. Nothing builds up integrity so quickly as another person's faith in you.

There will be times when children unconsciously plagiarize. This, rather than being termed a deliberate act of plagiarism, should be used for generalized discussion of the difference between an original and a copy. Help them to see clearly that out of their own experiences, redefined and rearranged, will come an expression that cannot possibly be mistaken for someone else's because it will be indelibly stamped with their own individuality.

TIME IS WHAT YOU HAVE

How ridiculous to say you have time! But you do. You always have time for the things you really value. Teaching boys and girls is an all-encompassing, enervating business from which you and they need the relief of enchantment. A few minutes for the "quiet mind," the "white space"—time for reflection. This is all the time you need, for as ideas commence to flow you are needed by your pupils less and less. With your fingers on the pulse of the situation you can go about your business of teaching a group here, providing materials there, giving a verbal pat on the back to one child, checking upon skills with another. All of these things you would be doing anyway, and the only difference really is that here and there in spots is "genius at work."

As freedom develops so, too, does self-direction. The faster you can work yourself out of a job, the more desirable it is. Since there is never enough time for all the things you need to do, each "self-starter" you get into motion gives you more time for all those other jobs.

Don't neglect that quiet time, for those ten minutes may be the key to the whole situation. As the day progresses, children will express their ideas with various media. Another few minutes at the end of the period or day for showing and evaluating what they've done will round off a working session and set the stage for the future.

Time? Well, time is only relative, and what you do with what you have is up to you.

LEAD BY FOLLOWING

The difference between suggesting things for children *to do* and putting them in contact with materials or ideas that stimulate their imaginations and encourage experimentation is so slight that one must constantly be on guard lest he suggest patterns. Too many materials or ways of expression may be confusing, lack of the right incentive at the right time may forestall some expression coming to the threshold. Here it is important to follow up leads and always have other possibilities at hand so that there is an opportunity to grope if need be. Again, knowing the children's interests, their levels of maturity, their potentialities, helps the teacher to know just how much to say or how many materials to provide to fan the embers into glowing flames. Following their leads you will ask questions that will carry them forward in the direction of their own thinking. It is seldom good to say "Why don't you try it this way?" It is often good to say "How do you think you can do it or say it?" The first question is giving leads, the second one is following theirs.

Lead by following. Good leadership has always been just that. The right question at the right time, a sensitivity to people's strengths and weaknesses, the just right word of encouragement, the summarizing of possible choices, helping persons find alternatives and having infinite faith in people and what they can accomplish. In teaching, leadership lies in knowing when to show or tell or instruct, and when just to let them muddle through. In releasing creative ideas, leadership means weeding and cultivating the soil so that the thought is not choked back by the weeds and does not die for lack of sun, air, or rain.

IT IS BETTER TO HAVE FAILED
THAN NEVER TO HAVE TRIED AT ALL

If one truly talented child is discovered through creative activities it will have been worth the trying. If one unhappy "tied-up-in-knots" child finds release and escape through some medium your interest will not have been in vain. If one child who has found success nowhere else finds it in creating, your efforts will not have been wasted. If one child *really* sees a sunset, hears the song of a lark, smells heather, touches the peach down, tastes the fog—you have earned a "well done." Par on this course for products is low; but par is high in that everyone who is exposed to beauty, everyone who is encouraged to see, hear, smell, touch and taste life in all of its exciting facets, has gained something from the experience. Every child who has enjoyed a quiet time, a time for meditation, a time for savoring experiences has found perhaps a little island of peace in a troubled world.

If you believe that children need *competence* in the *skills* of living and *confidence* for the *living*, you will be as concerned about creative living as you are about skill mastery, precision timing, and necessary conformity.

Yes, it is better to try, if you believe, for you cannot completely fail and you may accomplish a great deal. A balance for you? Today you win, tomorrow you lose. Even your favorite champion doesn't win all of the time.

THEY MUST MUDDLE THROUGH

Experimentation is the keynote. For every successful invention there are probably a hundred tries. For every poem, story, oil painting, building design or ballet there is usually a history of years of experimenting and putting different elements together to make a satisfying whole. Children *must* try things out. They *must* test the medium, whatever, it is, to discover its limits, its possibilities. How will they know it won't work if they don't try? Don't fancy that your own personal experiences will prove a thing to them. Naturally they build on what others have discovered to some extent, but plucking the strings of the violin, discovering pitch in various sizes of nails or water glasses, rolling words around on their tongues, testing liquids and solids and temperatures, finding the uses of tools—these and many other things they must do for themselves. School isn't the only place most of them will experiment, but it will be the only place where some children will have this opportunity.

Experimenting just for the sake of experimenting should not be forbidden. Sometimes in our frugal school-teacher way we worry about waste—wasted paper, wasted paints, wasted electricity, wasted time. It is right that we should teach and practice thrift. This is an age of too much of so many things for so many children. But when is waste *not* waste?

The answer to this conundrum is to be found in your sense of values. It is to be found in your judgment of what it is your

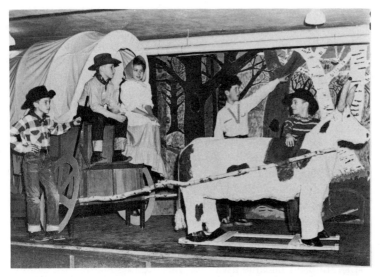

Planning, playing, evaluating

children need most. If a certain expensive drug may save a child's life you don't buy a cheaper product at a chain store or refuse to buy at all. It is your decision and your responsibility as to which is more important: a free-wheeling, free-thinking individual who rejoices in experimenting, or one who is afraid to try, afraid he may make a mistake, afraid he'll spoil something.

YOU, AGAIN

It's been a long road, a hard road. Going hasn't always been smooth. Take a hindsight view—from June back to September.

In September you were groping for ways to help every child operate at his highest efficiency level. You were fumbling for ways to develop integrity, self-confidence, imagination, tolerance, the scientific method, mutual respect and understanding, and automation. You knew then that the only road to these end-results lay in developing self-direction and self-discipline. The range of variability among the children in these traits was incredibly wide. You knew that the range would be as wide or wider in June, but you also knew that your goal was to help every child move at his own rate toward greater maturity.

So you set the stage. Slowly and thoughtfully you introduced new techniques, new materials, new ways of working. You recognized that without skills the children would wander around in a morass of ineffectuality. You knew that most of the time in your school day children would be involved in developing the skills, knowledge, and attitudes necessary for self-realization, human relationships, economic efficiency, and civic responsibility. You realized, however, that in order for these outcomes to be really achieved they needed to be practiced independently in small groups and by individuals. Their freedom had to be earned by demonstrating their sense of responsibility.

As you constantly used a few minutes a day to develop values —through poetry, prose, science, dancing, painting, melodies —the children became aware of varying media, varying avenues of creative thought. Gradually children began to break away from these mutual experiences as the planets from the sun, sometimes singly and sometimes in groups to try out their ideas. Business proceeded as usual, but more and more children began to use their free time to create. Sometimes after an aesthetic experience so many wanted to try their hands at some creative process that only a few were left for the teacher to supervise in drills and skills. Sometimes when many needed quiet, they practically hung out a sign: "Quiet, genius at work." But this was only "once in a while" and more often than not self-propelled groups or individuals set themselves apart on their own islands while the busy tide of the workaday world rose and ebbed around them. When children forgot their responsibilities they were gently reminded that first things must come first and that at times the teacher needed to be the judge of what the child needed most.

But now it is June. Everywhere there is evidence that children have been writing, painting, sculpturing, dramatizing, dancing, playing instruments, and experimenting with scientific principles.

On this particular day the room is alive with activity. A

group is painting a backdrop sketched by one child for the culminating program of their social studies unit. The theme is the universe. Another group is practicing the choral speaking of a poem written by the child who is directing them. Another group, to the chords of the autoharp and the bong-bong of the drums, is dancing the sun, moon, and stars with meteors and satellites. Still another group practices an original song. One child is sewing on a simple costume, another one practices a prologue, several boys are constructing some props for the stage.

You move quietly from group to group, from child to child, giving a word of encouragement here, materials there, answering their questions and pausing to ask them questions when evaluations are being made. No "canned" play is being performed here with parts and directions carefully typed out and assigned by the teacher. The enterprise has grown from many individual and group ideas. There are so many kinds of creative activity represented here that it is impossible to catalogue them all.

But even more important than this group project is the evidence of stories, poetry, paintings, drawings, paper sculpture, construction work, science experiments, musical and rhythmical instruments that are not even remotely related to the class project. There is a channel for each child, and even if he hasn't discovered it yet—he will. You can't hope to succeed with all children, but where you fail, the next teacher may succeed. A visitor in the classroom would immediately know that here creativity is prized, here uniqueness is sought after and cherished when it appears. This is a good spot because

> Everyone, everything, *each* thing is different, so that
> it isn't safe to know. You—you have to grope.[1]

[1] Rumer Godden, *An Episode of Sparrows* (New York: The Viking Press, Inc.; Toronto: The Macmillan Co. of Canada, Ltd., 1955), p. 199

Index